TABLE OF CONTENTS

ACRONYMS

AAR	After Action Review
COIN	Counterinsurgency
NGO	Non-governmental organization
FET	Female Engagement Team
U.S.	United States
ANP	Afghan National Police
ISAF	International Security Forces Afghanistan
PRT	Provincial Reconstruction Team

CHAPTER 1

INTRODUCTION

Atop the commanding Lieutenant Colonel's desk at the Counterinsurgency

(COIN) Training Center at Camp Julien, near Kabul, Afghanistan, a screen saver displays

the tanned buttocks of a bikini-clad woman. A journalist snapped a shot of this screen

saver and included it as part of an internet series, "Life, Death, and the Taliban" (Sennott

2009). One thoughtful blogger, a Marine deploying to Afghanistan observed, "I find this

photo reflective of what will become the most difficult paradigm shift for the uniformed

services; the role of women in securing the state . . . this photo is not only insulting for all

the obvious reasons, it is an indicator of something much deeper that longs to be

addressed" (Sennott 2009).

The blogger was calling for the United States (U.S.) military to take women more

seriously and to recognize the potential impact that Afghan women can make in helping

to counter the ongoing insurgency in Afghanistan.

According to U.S. military doctrine, to win at COIN, one has to win the support

of the people (U.S. Army 2006). This is because an insurgency does not have the

financial or other means to wage a full-scale war without relying on the local population

for food, money, weapons, shelter, and other logistics (Hand 2007). Responsible for

multiple tasks, including raising children, cooking, fetching water, farming, and taking

care of livestock, rural Afghan women are at the center of village life and know all of the

goings-on of their communities. Thus, they are valuable sources of intelligence regarding

insurgent activity in their villages and can offer important insight into the unmet

1

development and security needs of their communities (Matt Pottinger 2010). This information is critical to U.S. efforts to win the support of the Afghan people and drive out the Taliban and other insurgents.

Unfortunately, a prevalent perception within the U.S. military of Afghan women is that they are in a constant state of hidden bondage--inaccessible to outsiders and irrelevant even if they can be reached (Valerie M. Hudson 2010). This has resulted in their needs and insights being largely overlooked. Even though U.S. military doctrine specifically notes that women are "hugely influential" in forming the social networks that insurgents use for support (U.S. Army 2009), non-governmental organizations (NGO), journalists, academics, and veterans of the war in Afghanistan have all noted that this important principle has been an afterthought of the U.S. military's COIN strategy. After nearly a decade in Afghanistan, the U.S. Marine Corps has realized the folly of engaging only half the population and has institutionalized formal Female Engagement Teams (FETs). While these teams enjoy high-profile media coverage, they constitute only a fraction of U.S. COIN efforts and strategy.

Former Secretary of State Condoleezza Rice noted that, "In the dynamic 21st century, no society can expect to flourish with half its people sitting on the sidelines, with no opportunity to develop their talents, to contribute to their economy, or to play an equal part in the lives of their nations" (Rice 2006). The U.S. military should advance and implement a similar paradigm--that no COIN strategy whose success relies on the popular support of a community can expect to succeed if the women are left sitting on the sidelines. In short, the U.S. military needs to implement an Equal Opportunity COIN strategy.

The U.S. military teeters on verge of embracing such an idea but continues to approach the topic gingerly. General Stanley McChrystal has approved forty female Marines to deploy as attachments with an all-male infantry for the express purpose of gaining the trust of Afghan women (Bumiller 2010). Such small-scale programs need to be folded into mainstream COIN strategy and tactics and embraced as experiential, not experimental. U.S. doctrine finds that women are the foundation of social and economic networks that eventually undermine the insurgents (U.S. Army 2009), but this little-known gem needs to be highlighted and taught as a core COIN strategy, not forgotten in the annex of a COIN manual. Furthermore, the U.S. needs to re-vamp its efforts to address the known concerns of women, particularly in the area of security. With former mujahedeen staffing the ranks of 70 percent of Afghanistan's corrupt police force (Clark 2006), it is no surprise that women tolerate alternative guarantees from the Taliban as a better hedge for the safety and security of themselves and their children.

The essence of COIN is to focus on people, not just men. While Afghan village elders may purport to speak for entire communities, Afghan women tell human rights groups that these same elders come under pressure from insurgents to enforce their demands to restrict women's freedom of movement and the right to work (Reid 2010). As part of an Equal Opportunity COIN strategy, it is critical for U.S. military commanders to recognize the importance of women in re-building Afghanistan's society and integrate their concerns into military lines of operation.

Chapter 2 of this monograph will lay out existing literature in the following areas: COIN theory, the progress of governance, security, and U.S. reconstruction efforts in Afghanistan, the current security needs of Afghan women, the hidden power of Afghan women, and linkages between women and COIN. Chapter 3 will detail the research methodology used. Chapter 4 will propose that the U.S. military adopt an "equal opportunity" COIN strategy, and analyze how leveraging Afghan women can result in a more effective COIN. It will use a case study of a Female Engagement Team (FET) team to highlight this point and go on to suggest some key tasks that should be integrated into International Security Forces Afghanistan's (ISAF) three existing lines of operation–Security, Governance, and Development. Chapter 5 will highlight further recommendations for the U.S. military in developing an Equal Opportunity COIN strategy, and chapter 6 will offer a summarization and conclude the essential characteristics of the Equal Opportunity COIN.

CHAPTER 2

LITERARY REVIEW

The following titles theorize that insurgencies require the support of the local

populace in order to be defeated. This theme of population-centric COIN was enshrined

in the Department of the Army's Field Manual 3-24, *Counterinsurgency*, in 2006.

Manolis Priniotakis's, *Countering Insurgency and Promoting Democracy* (New York:

Council for Emerging National Security Affairs 2007) explains that insurgencies are

usually weaker than their enemies, which are normally a conventional government force.

The insurgent relies on the people to provide logistical support in the way of food,

shelter, training, clothing, ammunition, funds, etc. If the local populace opts not to

support the insurgent, these logistics dry up. COIN, therefore, requires co-opting the local

populace not to side with the insurgent. For the counterinsurgent, this co-opting of the

local populace not to side with the insurgent is as important, if not more important, than

defeating the insurgent militarily. Fawad Sediqi's Master's Thesis, "Why are the Taliban

still a Challenge for the Afghan Government and the International Community after their

Removal from Power?" (University of Kent, Canterbury 2009) emphasizes that in order

to co-opt the population, the counterinsurgent has to provide adequate security for the

population, or else the population will seek that security from the insurgent. Similarly, if

the counterinsurgents are unable to provide basic human services to the people, the

people will not perceive them as legitimate and may continue their support for the

insurgent. Therefore, it is critical for the counterinsurgent to both promise and deliver

guarantees for the human security and basic needs of the population. General Peter

5

W.Chiarelli's article, "Winning the Peace: The Requirement for Full Spectrum Operations" (*Military Review* (July/August 2005) highlights that security is more complicated than simply putting guns on every street corner. The root causes of insecurity that result from the absence of governance also need to be addressed.

Several titles assess the progress of governance, security, and U.S. reconstruction efforts in Afghanistan. Robert Crews', *The Taliban and the Crisis in Afghanistan* (Cambridge, MA 2008) and Kenneth Katzman's, *Afghanistan: Post-war Governance, Security, and U.S. Policy* (Washington, DC 2006) provide a broad snapshot of the country. They identify incremental progress regarding U.S. and coalition efforts to provide increased security, governance, rule of law, and infrastructure for the people of Afghanistan, set in the context of a generally volatile and non-permissive security environment. The Congressionally-mandated U.S. Department of Defense, *Report on Progress Toward Security and Stability in Afghanistan*, (April 2010) notes the strong and viable presence of an insurgency, as well the inability of Afghanistan's central government to provide effective security or provide essential human services for the majority of the population. It also highlights that, "The insurgents perceive 2009 as their most successful year." Furthermore, "A ready supply of recruits is drawn from the frustrated population, where insurgents exploit poverty, tribal friction, and lack of governance to grow their ranks." International Crisis Group's March 2003 report notes that Afghanistan's capital, Kabul, has benefitted the most from the U.S. and coalition presence in the way of increased security and humanitarian services delivery.

Several titles assess the most urgent human security challenges Afghan women confront, and their security prospects following a drawdown of U.S. troops in 2011.

Rachel Reids 24 February 2010 Congressional testimony on behalf of the NGO Human Rights Watch notes incremental improvements for women in the areas of education, human rights, and access to basic health and human services. The United Nations Assistance Mission in Afghanistan report, *Silence is Violence: End the Abuse of Women in Afghanistan* (Geneva: Office of the United Nations High Commissioner for Human Rights 2009) cautions that the progress Afghan women have made with the support of the international community is eroding under a stronger Taliban presence, coupled with the presence of former warlords in positions of legitimacy and power under the regime of Afghanistan's President Hamid Karzai. Valerie M. Hudson and Patricial Leidl's article, "Betrayed", published in *Foreign Policy* magazine (10 May 2010) stresses that Afghan women feel forgotten and left out of the negotiations underway to integrate "moderate" Taliban into mainstream governance. The authors express concern that Afghanistan's new leadership is making important political decisions about the future of Afghanistan without making any commitment to address endemic violence and discrimination against Afghan women, and that the withdrawal of U.S. and coalition forces will leave behind an Afghan government that is just as corrupt, misogynistic, and hostile to protecting women's rights as the Taliban government was.

Several titles offer anecdotal and anthropological insight into the ability of Afghan women to use gender-centric networks to socialize, organize, and resist against oppression. Cheryl Bernard's *Veiled Courage: Inside the Afghan Women's Resistence*, (New York: Broadway Books 2002) emphasizes that the stereotypical image of Afghan women as meek, pliable, and irrelevant in revolution and resistance is not accurate. Anne E. Brodsky's, *With all our Strength: The Revolutionary Association of the Women of*

7

Afghanistan, explains how the suffering and oppression of Afghan women as a result of over thirty years of war has created women who leverage whatever strength and resources they can to make incremental gains in their human rights, access to education, and access to economic opportunity. Deborah Rodriguez's, *Kabul Beauty School: An American Woman goes Behind the Veil,* (Ashland, OR, 2007) chronicles the author's story opening a beauty school in Kabul for Afghan women. Her narrative helps to dispel the notion that Afghan women are powerless and need to be "saved". Rather, Afghan women need partners and allies who are willing to engage them and recognize the potential they have to contribute to their country if consulted, heard, and assisted in their efforts to secure political, economic, and social inclusion.

Several titles highlight the important role that women play in both supporting and countering insurgencies. Matt Pottinger, Hali Jilani, and Claire Russo's article, "Half-Hearted: Trying to Win Afghanistan without Afghan Women." (*Small Wars Journal* 2010) explains how women are at the center of village life and valuable sources of intelligence for counterinsurgents. Further, it emphasizes that the perception of Afghan women as powerless in their homes is incorrect, and in fact, women have a large influence on their families in Pashtun culture. MAJ Mona Jibril, Director of the Non-Governmental Assistance Center, Iraq, gave an interview to the U.S. Army Combat Studies Institute on 20 December 2006 and explains that the central role as caregiver means that women are inclined to seek peaceful solutions to conflict in the interest of their families. In addition, she explains how women create social and economic networks that help to defeat insurgencies neighborhood by neighborhood. In the U.S. Army Field Manual 3-24.2, *Tactics in Counterinsurgency*, U.S. military doctrine suggests targeting these networks by proactively engaging women and turning them against insurgents. Further, U.S. military doctrine emphasizes that women have influence within the family unit, and that positively influencing women leads to positively influencing children, families, and eventually communities.

CHAPTER 3

METHDOLOGY

This monograph relies upon qualitative research and analysis. This type of analysis uses critical thinking to analyze a problem by collecting information from multiple sources. The sources include both primary and secondary materials as follows:

Military: U.S. Army doctrine, primary-source U.S. military analysis, including "lessons learned" reports, after-action reviews (AAR's), and operational leadership experiences conducted by the U.S. Army Combat Studies Institute.

Academic: Journal articles, books, and other scholarly literature and excerpts from speaking engagements from experts in political science, women's studies, developmental economics, COIN and Afghanistan.

Government: Reports produced by U.S. federal agencies and remarks given by current and former senior-level U.S. political and military leaders at public functions.

Media: Media stories from major news outlets.

Advocacy documents: Excerpts from political and advocacy documents from international governmental organizations, NGO, and Afghan women's advocacy groups.

The research question to be answered in this monograph is whether U.S. and coalition forces recognize the importance of engaging the women of Afghanistan in their COIN strategy. An analysis of the above-referenced source material will explain the root causes of insurgency in Afghanistan, demonstrating that insurgency is rooted in the failure of the Government of Afghanistan, in conjunction with U.S. and coalition forces to provide adequate security and services for the Afghan people, fueling support for

10

alternative security guarantees from the Taliban and other insurgent groups. Further analysis reveals that although Afghan women can be a powerful force against insurgency, their value has historically been ignored or disregarded because of an almost universal perception that they are both powerless and irrelevant in Afghan society. As a result, their security needs have been largely unmet and are particularly acute. Based on these analyses, as well as anecdotal evidence from military servicemen and women, this monograph asserts that Afghan women need to be leveraged by U.S. and coalition forces in order to defeat the insurgency and bring about more peace and stability in Afghanistan.

This thesis asserts that U.S. military and coalition forces have grasped the significance of Afghan women in countering insurgency only anecdotally, but overall, an Equal Opportunity COIN strategy needs to be adopted. This strategy calls for the following:

Recognition that in a people-centric COIN, ignoring half the population means missing significant opportunities to gain intelligence and build trust within Afghan communities.

Recognition that the notion that Afghan women are powerless in Afghan society is not necessarily correct.

Recognition that Afghan women, as the primary care-givers in their families, are at the center of village life. As such, they are not only valuable sources of intelligence for counterinsurgents, but they are also a key population whose trust must be earned and respected in order to help win the community's support against insurgents.

Recognition that it is not necessarily consistent with Afghan "culture" to severely repress women and prevent them from access to personal security, rule of law, education,

11

and economic opportunity. Rather, the status of women in Afghanistan has never been static and is largely dictated by the political agenda of whoever is in power in Afghanistan.

Recognition that while Afghan women come from conservative backgrounds and their movements and personal freedoms are restricted, the U.S. military and coalition forces can and should think creatively about how to access this key population.

Recognition that ISAF's lines of operation, namely security, governance, and development, need to include women-centric tasks in order to have a truly Equal Opportunity COIN.

CHAPTER 4

ANALYSIS

After eight years of engagement with the Afghans, someone has finally realized
that we have been missing out on 50% of the population who have an enormous
influence within the family and especially on adolescent males who make up the
recruiting pool of the insurgents.

—Blog entry by Lt. Col J.J. Malevich, Director of Counterinsurgency, United States
Army/United States Marine Corps Counterinsurgency Center, 2009

<u>Why Afghan Women are missing in U.S. Counterinsurgency efforts</u>

Counterinsurgency doctrine has emerged as a popular and relevant consideration

in warfare. The U.S. experience in Afghanistan and Iraq since 11 September 2001 has

forced military planners to seriously examine why the world's most sophisticated and

superior military forces have not yet defeated an enemy that fights with little more than

Kalashnikovs and improvised explosive devices. The most recent U.S. Army/Marine

Corps Counterinsurgency Field Manual, released in 2006 to equip U.S. troops with

updated doctrinal guidance, explains that, "at its core, COIN is a struggle for the

population's support. The protection, welfare, and support of the people are vital to

success" (U.S. Army 2006). Furthermore, "Whatever else is done, the focus must remain

on gaining and maintaining the support of the population. With their support, victory is

assured; without it, COIN efforts cannot succeed" (U.S. Army 2006). An insurgency does

not have the popular, financial, or organizational means to support a full-scale war. The

insurgent's military weakness compels him to maintain the support of the people in order

to succeed (Hand 2007). These COIN principles stem from China's infamous Communist leader Mao Zedong, who noted that, "revolutionary forces are the fish and the people the sea in which they swim" (Mao Tse-Tung n.d.). Mao theorized that fighting a COIN assumed that guerrillas, weaker than their enemies, could not survive without strong, well-organized popular support.

In Afghanistan, a high illiteracy rate necessitates that winning the support of the people must happen via direct communication with local leaders (Roberts 2005). It is more likely than not that the communication with local leaders will be with Afghan men. This is because Afghan men are the face of the traditional tribal power structures. At village and sub-district levels, authority is grounded in tribal structures and exercised through village councils (shuras) traditionally open only to men (International Crisis Group 2003). Pashtun society, in particular, has strong rules and morals, enforced, sometimes brutally, at the family and tribal levels when it comes to the interaction of their women with men (Krawchuk 2007). Because access to women is difficult, and the inappropriate handling of situations involving women can cause deep seeded and lasting animosity, U.S. forces are limited in their capability to reach out to women in their COIN efforts. The problem, however, is that difficult as they are to access, women still make up fifty percent of Afghanistan's population and are valuable sources of information and public opinion. Says noted Afghanistan expert Lester W. Grau, "Afghan women are the keepers of the flame. They know everything going on in the village. They are also the most difficult for outsiders to reach" (Grau 2010). Notes CNN, "The Marines mostly operate in the more rural, conservative areas in southern Afghanistan. There, men are not allowed to look at–let alone talk to–women. So the predominantly male Marine units were missing a chance to engage 50 percent of the Afghan people" (Lawrence 2010).

14

Many battlefield commanders also assume engaging local women will pay no dividend, and they are not willing to commit the necessary personnel resources to tap this hard-to-access element of the population (Matt Pottinger 2010).

Therefore, the enormous challenge of engaging Afghan women falls upon a very small player in the overall U.S. COIN strategy–the Provincial Reconstruction Team (PRT). This hybrid civilian-military mechanism delivers small village improvement projects to establish good relations with Afghans and collect intelligence on local events and personalities (Perito 2005). On 26 May 2007, PRT development projects were worth only $630 million (Afghan Women's Network 2007), as compared to the overall U.S. military budget for Afghanistan of 47 billion dollars in 2009, and 65 billion dollars in 2010 (Tyson 2009). Although specifically required "to endeavor to have a gender component" (Afghan Women's Network 2007) the PRTs sometimes do not consistently inform or include Afghan women in development projects (Afghan Women's Network 2007).

Pressure from senior military authorities to demonstrate progress, coupled with limited knowledge of local conditions has resulted in PRT consultations with all-male village elders to bring an infrastructure project that is often costly and impossible for Afghans to maintain (Jones 2009). With speed being the priority, the results are often hastily constructed buildings (Perito 2005). A comprehensive report from the United States Institute for Peace notes, "Schools were built without teachers and clinics without doctors. Multiple wells dried up shallow aquifers. With few, if any, technical criteria, some of the construction was substandard" (Perito 2005).

When women are invited to participate in PRT activities, it is sometimes impossible for them to do so due to security constraints (Afghan Women's Network 2007). Despite the importance of establishing a stable environment in Afghanistan, the security role assigned to PRTs is only to provide for their own protection (Perito 2005). PRTs are not responsible for protecting Afghans, excluded from conducting activities in the counternarcotics effort, and not expected to track and engage insurgents (Perito 2005). The mission of the armed element in the PRTs is limited to protection of their own forces, in other words providing armed escorts for the PRT's commander and civilian members (Perito 2005). Genevieve Chase, a well-known veteran, activist and Pashtun-language specialist who survived a suicide attack in Afghanistan sums up the problem, asking, "Why build schools, provincial centers, bridges and wells, when there is no support or security provided for villages to utilize them?" (Ree 2009).

A successful Equal Opportunity COIN strategy recognizes that, while difficult for the U.S. military to access, Afghan women are half the population. Failure to develop strategies to engage them means the intelligence, insights, and inputs of half the population will literally be ignored by the counterinsurgent.

Why Women Matter in Counterinsurgency

Many battlefield commanders assume engaging local women will pay no dividend, and they are not willing to commit the necessary personnel resources to tap this hard-to-access element of the population (Matt Pottinger 2010). An April 2009 comprehensive document chronicling reports, lessons and observations from 2007-2009 in Afghanistan reflects this. Of its 367 pages, it dedicates one small section to the role of women in Afghanistan, only to conclude that

16

[I]n most rural Pashtun communities, women live completely hidden lives inside their father's or their husband's *Qalat*, or high-walled mud compound. . . . As a result of this state of hidden bondage, women play no part whatever in either insurgency and there are no women in either the Taliban or *Hizb-i-Islami* Gulbuddin (HiG). (United States Marine Corps Center for Lessons Learned 2009)

In light of intelligence such as this, it is not surprising, though not unfortunate, that the mainstream perception in the U.S. military, and indeed in most of the U.S., is that Afghan women are largely irrelevant to coalition efforts to build trust and make in-roads in Afghan communities. Yet a closer look at accounts from academics, journalists, and military personnel reveals that this is simply not true.

In fact, women willingly and unwillingly fill a variety of roles within insurgent organizations. These roles include providing moral and logistics support, including time, sewing, food, supplies, and safe haven, in the organization (Sutten 2009). They are also a large part of undermining insurgency-insurgencies are built neighborhood by neighborhood like gangs and if the women resist, the men resist too (Jibril 2006).

Contrary to popular perception, women are active and relevant in the Afghan home and play a critical role in their society (Skaine 2002). Credited for helping to found the Marine Corps first FET team, then Lt. Pottinger noted in 2009, "Despite their traditional status as second class citizens, even when compared to Arab women, Pashtun women still wield influence over their husbands and especially their children" (Pottinger 2009). In a subsequent article, Pottinger notes that,

Rural Pashtun women are responsible for raising children, collecting water, cooking, and helping farm and care for animals, among other jobs. Though rarely seen by outsiders, they are keen observers and opinion-makers about the goings-on in their villages. "The women pass all the news in the villages," says an Afghan National Army colonel who cautions against ignoring half the country's population. "They know who is doing what, who should and should not be in the area. They talk around the well or while they are collecting firewood about the news they have heard from their husbands [and their kids]." (Matt Pottinger 2010)

Lieutenant Colonel .J.J. Malevich, Director of the COIN, U.S. Army/U.S. Marine

Corps COIN Center muses in a December 2009 blog,

> In 2005, I was sitting under a tree at Shira, in Kapisa Province with Minister Stanakzia who was in charge of the Disarmament of Illegally Armed Groups program. I was struck by the fact that there were no women to be seen anywhere. I mentioned this to the Minister and he explained to me that although there were no women present, in Afghan culture they were quite powerful in the home. (Malevich 2009)

Six years before Pottinger and his team institutionalized the FET teams, another

serviceman published some observations: "Sometimes I see women peering out from the

corners of their homes, interested in what we are. They send their kids to wave or try to

speak English, but they stay hidden" (Roberts 2005). He writes another letter to his wife

noting,

> Had another good day yesterday. We went to a clinic and a couple schools…We had a female Afghan-American [interpreter] with us and the girls were all agog – seeing a woman dressed in DCUs and Flak vest talking Pashto. Got some good information and made some more contacts. This is a battle, so you have to make friends and get as much info to get a good picture of what is happening. The surface is rarely the truth. (Roberts 2005)

Roberts was not attempting to draw any cultural or anthropological conclusions

about the status of women in Pashtun culture, but his vignette evinces that while women

are not necessarily free to engage servicemen openly, they are certainly involved and

curious about the goings-on in their community and can exert influence and even

hospitality using their children as their proxies.

Major Mona Jibril, director of the NGO Assistance Center in Iraq in 2004 shares

profound experiences with Iraqi women, noting, "One of the things I really missed in

Iraq--and wished I'd seen earlier and incorporated into my directorship of the NGO

assistance center--was how important and how influential the women are in Iraqi society.

18

I didn't get it until almost the very end, and it's so easy to forget" (Jibril 2006). She goes

on to observe,

> Women carry life and are always interested in the family unit. They will sacrifice themselves for their children, irrespective of culture or religion. Women are much more interested in peace and peaceful solutions than they are in combative solutions. They will make things work whereas the men would rather kill each other or solve things by violent means. Women, however, will work it out–and I didn't get this until the very end. The female-run NGOs were actually the best funded, the best organized and got the most done. They're amazing and strong people, and we could have made so many more inroads with the NGOs if we had looked at that. (Jibril 2006)

While the Afghan household might constitute a place of oppressive social

relations for women in terms of hard, unpaid labor and domestic violence, the home still

represents a place of personal fulfillment and meaningful social relations, resources and

status for women (Standal 2008). It is shortsighted, therefore, to assume that because the

Afghan woman has a repressed status in the public sphere, that she is therefore irrelevant

in the private sphere. Women's space to participate in community decision-making is

contingent on their space in decision-making within the family and marriage relationship.

The family constitutes the micro-level where the rules and mobility of each individual in

the family is formed. The gender relations within the family are a result of negotiation,

and this negotiation takes place continuously through both household and community

discourse (Standal 2008). There is space for the U.S. military to insert itself in the

community-level discourse, and some innovative commanders have already done so

through informal mechanisms. If done with the proper resources, thought, training,

preparation, and planning, the U.S. military can leverage the community discourse to

build the trust of Afghan women, and as U.S. military doctrine points out, "Win the

19

women, and you own the family unit. Own the family, and you take a big step forward in mobilizing the population" (U.S. Army 2009).

Marsha Michel, a field officer for the U.S. Agency for International Development and FET team coordinator for Afghan's Farah province writes, "Even before getting to Afghanistan people would tell me it would be difficult to work with the women here because of cultural customs. After only a few months of being here I realized that women here just need a little direction, and an opportunity to showcase their skills." (Darius 2010)

Michel's observation is important because it addresses a potential criticism of the Equal Opportunity COIN principle–namely that making contact with Afghan women and addressing their needs and concerns as they pertain to their security and access to justice, education, and employment is somehow contrary to Afghan culture. Yet, before the Taliban came to power, Afghan women composed 50 percent of government workers, 70 percent of schoolteachers and 40 percent of doctors in Kabul (United Nations Development Fund for Women n.d.). A May 2010 article in Foreign Policy magazine, penned by an Afghan expatriot, notes wistfully,

> A half-century ago, Afghan women pursued careers in medicine; men and women mingled casually at movie theaters and university campuses in Kabul; factories in the suburbs churned out textiles and other goods. There was a tradition of law and order, and a government capable of undertaking large national infrastructure projects, like building hydropower stations and roads, albeit with outside help. Ordinary people had a sense of hope, a belief that education could open opportunities for all, a conviction that a bright future lay ahead. All that has been destroyed by three decades of war, but it was real. (Qayoumi 2010)

The author compiled an astounding photo essay documenting some of these observations. Nearly twenty black-and-white photos display Afghan women in stylish pencil-skirts, socializing with men, attending university, working in hospitals and laboratories (Qayoumi 2010). While these photos captured scenes from in and around Kabul and not in the more conservative countryside, they serve as an important reminder that the status of women in Afghan society is not static in Afghan culture. Rather, the role of women and their particiaption in Afghan society is a highly politicized issue that continues to change depending on the political environmnet. To form assumptions about Afghan women based exclusively on the current political climate in Afghanistan–which has been dictated for over thirty years by various groups of misogynistic warlarods, does not necessarily lend to accurate predictions about what is a culturally appropriate COIN effort should look like. An Equal Opportunty COIN strategy will understand that exisiting networks of power in Afghanistan may continue to insist on a status quo that perpetuates a policy of repression for Afghan women. The equal opportunity counterinsurgent will look for culturally sensitive ways to engage women directly, as the U.S. Marine Corps has begun doing with FET's.

A successful Equal Opportunity COIN strategy recognizes that Afghan women are not irrelevant in the Afghan family. In fact, the opposite is often the case–Afghan women often wield significant influence in their families via their children. Further, engaging Afghan women in discussions about their needs regarding security, access to justice, education, and employment is not necessarily antithetical to Afghan culture. Afghan women have a long history in the participation of their communities.

Case Study--The Female Engagement Team

The experience of discrete military units in Afghanistan reveals that Afghan women can be valuable sources of intelligence, but also important mediums for the U.S.

military to build trust within a community–trust that contributes to the foundation of community support against an insurgency.

In early 2009, the Special Purpose Marine Air Ground Task Force-Afghanistan Ground Combat Element (Third Battalion, Eighth Marines) requested female Marines to support a cordon-and-knock operation in Farah Province. Third Battalion, Eighth Marines set up a cordon around a village in order to detain two men involved in Improvised Explosive Device attacks on Marines. After setting up the cordon, the on-scene commander spoke with the village elder and explained to him that the male Marines, accompanied by Afghan National Police (ANP), would like to search some homes. The commander also explained that the unit would do this without any male Marines coming into contact with local women (Pottinger 2009).

The village elder agreed to permit the unit to allow the female Marines to meet with the village women and distribute school supplies and hygiene products. This FET engaged in a lengthy discussion with the local women, distributed school supplies, and held informal classes on how to use some hygiene products and cosmetics. The team "spent hours chatting with the women and built an excellent rapport" (Pottinger 2009). The AAR notes that the event provided two significant benefits; it "gathered valuable information" and "it produced a victory from an information operations standpoint". The report goes on to say that, "the interaction with the local women, who had been clearly frightened when the Marines first arrived, ended up being extremely warm. The FET cast Coalition Forces in a positive light to a segment of the population that without the FET is beyond our ability to influence positively" (Pottinger 2009).

A few days later, the unit revisited the village. The on-site commander held a shura council with the village men to explain why the unit had detained two men, to reassure the attendees that the detainees would not be harmed, to reiterate the mission and resolve of the Marines in the area, and to distribute book-bags, school supplies, and some food. At the same time, the FET revisited all the local women to deliver a similar message and to distribute supplies. The AAR concludes, "We believe this follow-up mission helped to blunt local anger and to preserve the relationship between the FET and some of the local women" (Pottinger 2009).

The FET started out with intentions linked to cordon and search but placed a greater emphasis on information operations and substantive engagement with the female population. The AAR observes:

> Pashtun females in Afghanistan pose virtually no threat to Marines. While Iraqi women were sometimes employed by the insurgency as couriers, scouts, or even suicide bombers, there is little or no evidence that Pashtun women are employed in this manner by Afghan insurgents. This crucial difference in Pashtun and Arab culture liberates us to place a greater focus on proactively engaging Pashtun women than . . . in Iraq. (Pottinger 2009)

The ISAF covered the Marine's activities in Farah province, documenting some of the feedback in interviews. For example, Capt. Mike Hoffman, commanding officer of Company I, 3rd Bn., 8th Marines, noted "[The team] provides us access to half of the population that we normally do not have access to" (International Security Forces Afghanistan 2010). ISAF also observed, "Team leader, 2nd Lt. Johanna Shaffer, said their first mission, a cordon and search during Operation Pathfinder, was very successful. 'We were accepted by both the men and women villagers and were able to obtain valuable information about the way they lived and what they thought about the Marine Corps operating in the area.'"

23

Lt. Shaffer also makes a telling point that corroborates the multiplier effect

women have within the family unit, noting,

> Although Afghan women tend to be less outspoken than Afghan men, they have a large influence on their children. If the women know we are here to help them, they will likely pass that on to their children. If the children have a positive perspective of alliance forces, they will be less likely to join insurgent groups or participate in insurgent activities. (International Security Forces Afghanistan 2010)

Tom Ricks, a New York Times Reporter who closely follows this approach to

COIN expands on an AAR recommendation to use the FETs "to distribute grain directly

to the women of each household," noting the logic that taking humanitarian aid into the

compounds where the women can get it is preferable to "dumping it on a clamoring

crowd in the marketplace, where the strongest, fastest or most- feared men get it" (Ricks

2009).

The Marines' experience in Farah demonstrates that the Afghan FETs have the

potential, when well executed, to not only conduct security checks on females, but also to

gain insight into Afghan culture and build a sense of trust with a segment of the Afghan

population which has all too often been marginalized and ignored. The Marines deemed

the experience so significant in terms of collecting intelligence and conducting

information operations that the AAR made a critical recommendation as follows:

> We respectfully recommend that II MEB make active--even routine--use of Female Engagement Teams. The benefits (the acquisition of valuable information and the opportunity to positively influence an otherwise untouchable half of the local populace) clearly outweighed the primary cost (having to take a handful of female Marines from their regular billets on a periodic, temporary basis). (Pottinger 2009)

This was a forward-looking and practical observation about the potential that FETs have, which highlights the importance not simply of isolating women during a search, but also building trust with the other half of the population.

The Marine Corps had dabbled with outreach to women in Operation Iraqi Freedom, most notably with its 2008 Operation Lioness, in which female Marines participated in culturally-sensitive methods of searching Iraqi women to deter the enemy's use of females to conduct terrorist attacks. The Marine "Lioness" teams of Iraq had been successfully utilized to search female Iraqis for concealed weapons and contraband items during a wide variety of missions, including raids on houses and compounds, traffic control points, and voting registration drives. The Marine's experiences in Lioness, much like their experience in Farah, Afghanistan, turned up an unexpected benefit to engaging directly with the women (Latty 2009). The Marines noted, "When the locals see us they are interested because they don't see many females out on these missions. We use that interest to gain their trust or get perspectives that were unobtainable before" (Latty 2009).

As a result of these positive experiences, all international and Afghan security forces were ordered in November of 2009 to establish their own FET teams, with the commanding general of the International Security Assistance Force Joint Command signing an order calling on units to "create female teams to build relations with Afghan women" (Pottinger 2009).

The experience of the original FET teams, as well as those coming online in 2010, enjoy coverage from major media outlets, including *CNN*, the *New York Times*, and *NPR*.

The optimism and energy that comes from these units is palpable, and the military at the highest levels has recognized their utility.

A successful Equal Opportunity COIN strategy recognizes that with resources, effort, and creativity, the U.S. military can successfully engage Afghan women as part of its counterinsurgency tactics.

Tasks for a Gender-Balanced Counterinsurgency Strategy

However promising the prospect of FET teams, they represent only a tiny portion of the overall U.S. and coalition COIN strategy. Women have not been a central priority for the Afghan government or from coalition forces, whose focus is primarily on armed conflict rather than the broader concept of civilian security and rule of law (Reid 2010). In rural areas, where 74 percent of Afghans reside, it is estimated that 90 percent of women cannot read or write. 43 percent of females are less than 18 years when they marry. Afghanistan has one of the worst maternal mortality rates in the world-one woman dies every 27 minutes due to pregnancy-related complications (United Nations Assistance Mission in Afghanistan 2009). According to the 2007 Human Development Report, which measures education, longevity, and economic performance, Afghanistan ranked 174 out of 178 countries (United Nations Assistance Mission in Afghanistan 2009). A nationwide survey of 4,700 women, published in 2008, found that 87.2 percent had experienced at least one form of physical, sexual, or psychological violence or forced marriage in their lifetimes (Reid 2010).

In response to the collective failings of their countrymen and the international community to address these urgencies, in a note to diplomats and military leaders ahead of the London Conference on Afghanistan on 28 January 2010, Afghan women leaders

laid out specific concerns they felt were not being met.

> Fundamental to progress in Afghanistan is enhanced security on the
> ground. But achieving true security will require more than military stabilization; it
> will require women's freedom of movement and access to basic services--police
> protection, justice, health care, education, and clean water. Additionally, it will
> necessitate social change in private as well as public life; rampant domestic
> violence and other abuses of women's rights exacerbated by conflict are major
> contributors to women's insecurity. Women experience instability differently
> from men; they therefore have specific perspectives on how to achieve security
> for all Afghan citizens. (Afghan Women's Network 2010)

These concerns can be broadly categorized into four areas of human security, all

of which are interrelated, and which can be easily folded into ISAF existing lines of

operation of security, governance, and development as key tasks (ISAF 2010). First,

women require personal security in order to ease constraints on their freedom of

movement. Violence against women, whether in the home or in public, is rampant.

Second, Afghan governance does not adequately protect women, Police and judges see

violence against women as legitimate, so they do not prosecute cases (Reid 2010).

Afghan women are supposed to be protected by the Afghan Constitution, but the equal

opportunity enshrined in that document exists more on paper than it does in reality.

Discrimination against Afghan women in law and in fact, and the U.S. plan to integrate

"moderate" Taliban back into governance structures means that women are at risk of

losing what personal freedoms they have gain since U.S. operations began in Afghanistan

in 2001. Third, women and girls continue to lack sufficient educational opportunities

(United Nations Assistance Mission in Afghanistan 2009). The absence of education

constrains women from participating fully in society, from reading price-tags in the

market to reading brochures about their children's health. Further, women's lack of education fuels insurgency, as uneducated women are less able to provide opportunity for their children, who turn to insurgents for livelihood, purpose, and direction (Kolenda 2010). The education issue is closely related to the security issue, as much of the time, educational access is limited due to security constraints (United Nations Assistance Mission in Afghanistan 2009). Fourth, women in Afghanistan lack economic opportunity, an issue exacerbated by lack of education. Exclusion from formal employment pushes women into illegal activities, like prostitution and drug trafficking, to support themselves and their families (International Crisis Group 2003). At best, these activities force women to rely on whatever anti-U.S. faction is currently providing security in their village. At worst, such activities actively fund and fuel insurgent activity. These three areas, personal security, governance, and access to education, are profoundly interrelated elements of an over-arching human security plan for Afghan women.

A successful Equal Opportunity COIN strategy should integrate a specific, women-centric focus into Operation Enduring Freedom's lines of operation by prioritizing some carefully thought-out stability tasks.

Task 1--Train Afghan National Police to Understand and Enforce Security for Women (Security Line of Effort)

A fundamental social pact between any modern government and its people is the provision of security. The theory is that man agrees to surrender his natural liberty in return for the protection of the State. In Afghanistan, insurgents have eroded peoples' faith in this contract by creating chaos and insecurity through strategically orchestrated attacks, which the weak central government cannot prevent. As fear and insecurity spread among the population, government legitimacy erodes, and the people of Afghanistan are forced to seek "alternative security guarantees" that insurgents are happy to provide in exchange for the support of their cause (Davidson 2007). If the Afghan government is unable to provide security to the people, the U.S. must do so; otherwise, the Taliban can easily inhabit the security vacuum left by the Afghan government.

The current U.S. strategy in Afghanistan is to accelerate the handing over of Afghan security to Afghan forces and allow the U.S. to begin the transfer of forces out of Afghanistan in July of 2011 (Clinton 2009). However, a key component of Afghanistan's new security force is the (ANP), which has been unable to establish law and order and provide security in the areas outside of Kabul. ANP members keep their allegiances to the local commanders, warlords, and tribal leaders because a major part of the ANP has been " . . . created out of the factional militias in 2002, with militia commanders becoming chiefs of police at the district or provincial level and their sub-commanders being appointed as officers" (Sediqi 2009). Unfortunately, the abusive behavior of police has turned much of the rural populace towards the Taliban (Sediqi 2009). In the Pankela village of Helmand province, for example, the Talban were welcomed by the locals to get rid of the corrupt police. The locals voiced their unhappiness about the local police and maintained, "for God's sake do not bring back the Afghan police "(Sediqi 2009). Thus, the ANP has not only been unable to establish law and order, but rather contributed to further fuel the insurgency and force the population to either mostly side with the Taliban or remain neutral and indifferent. This situation has negatively impacted the countryside and pushed the people to join the Taliban; one business owner stated that 'in our hearts we don't support the Taliban, but people have no choice because the government can't provide them with security" (Sediqi 2009). One senior diplomat described Afghan police simply as, "the providers of violence" (Clark 2006). In February of 2010, the Department of Defense began to take over training of the ANP because contractors hired by the U.S. Department of State failed to keep pace with the growing instability in Afghanistan or address the security needs of the civilian population (Novak 2010).

The threat of violence is an everyday concern for Afghan women, thus the ANP's failures impact women in particular (United Nations Assistance Mission in Afghanistan 2009). Rape and sexual violence, including in detention facilities, so-called "honor" killings, the exchange of women and girls as a form of dispute-resolution, trafficking and abduction, forced marriages, domestic violence, as well as threats or attacks against women in public life, are some of the problems many Afghan women endure (United Nations Assistance Mission in Afghanistan 2009). It is up to the local authorities as to whether women will have any redress or protection from these crimes.

Thus, Afghan women are concerned that the men who plan the country's future define "security" in ways that have nothing to do with them. Wherever troops advance in Afghanistan, women are caught in the cross-fire, killed, wounded, forced to flee or locked up once again, just as they were in the time of the Taliban (Jones 2009). Because of their violent past and equally violent present, many Afghan women do not equate "security" with the presence of armed men, particularly the ANP (Jones 2009).

Brigadier General Vance, former commander NATO JTF notes that "security at the end of a gun is not security, it is defense, and defense is not that impressive. Battlefield success does not equal mission success." (Vance 2010). A gun on every street corner provides only a short-term solution and does not equate to long term security grounded in a democratic process (Chiarelli 2005).

Task 2--Encourage and Identify Afghan Leadership that Committed to the Constitutionally-Guaranteed Rights of Afghan Women (Governance Line of Effort)

As the U.S. begins the process of drawing down its troop commitments in Afghanistan, political settlement with the Taliban and other insurgent groups is quickly becoming a core part of the exit strategy for U.S. and coalition forces (Reid 2010). The Afghan government has empowered current and former warlords, providing official positions to some and impunity to others (Reid 2010). The result has been a series of setbacks for Afghan women in terms of their rights, freedom, and safety. For example, in August of 2009, Afghanistan's President Hamid Karzai authorized a repressive law that formalizes discrimination against Shia women. Among other things, the law gives a husband the right to withdraw basic maintenance from his wife, including food, if she refuses to obey his sexual demands. It grants guardianship of children exclusively to their fathers and grandfathers. It requires women to get permission from their husbands to work. It also effectively allows a rapist to avoid prosecution by paying "blood money" to a girl who was injured when he raped her (Human Rights Watch 2010). The law was designed in secret by a powerful and hard-line Shia leader, Ayatollah Asif Mohseni, and supported by conservative Shia leaders in parliament. Many women activists and human rights organizations accused President Karzai of abandoning his previous moderate views on women's rights to help him secure votes in the August 2009 presidential election (Human Rights Watch 2010).

It is critical for coalition forces to remain mindful of the long history of misogyny women have suffered under the Taliban, other insurgent groups, and now-legitimate warlords alike and not to understate the threat facing women should those committed to

31

extremist ideologies be given power at the local, provincial or national levels (Reid 2010). Lest the U.S. agenda for women's empowerment take a back seat to the exigency of a coalition exit strategy, women should be included in the planning for this impending reintegration and reconciliation, the outcomes of which will impact them at every level. Rachel Reid, the senior Afghanistan analyst for the NGO Congressional testimony of Human Rights Watch notes,

> Many [Afghan] women expressed frustration that there is little transparency about the government's reintegration and reconciliation plans. They are well aware that initiatives and policies are currently being drawn up that will have enormous impact on them, but they have not been kept informed, let alone consulted. Women want to be included in a serious manner while they still have a chance to make recommendations and influence decisions. They also want to be represented in large numbers if a peace jirga takes place by women who will advocate their views and rights-not by what they fear may be compliant and token delegates. (Reid 2010)

It goes on to emphasize,

> As the United States decreases its troop commitments and political engagement in Afghanistan, it is important to recognize that the threat to women's rights comes from the Afghan government as well as former warlords, the Taliban, and other armed groups. Too often, politics trumps justice when women's rights are at stake. President Karzai's efforts to reach out to Taliban leaders cannot be an excuse to appease fundamentalist demands to oppress women. Afghan women were deeply disappointed that President Obama's December 2009 speech outlining a new US strategy for Afghanistan did not mention women. Similarly, women and girls were largely missing from the Afghanistan and Pakistan Stabilization Strategy released by the Office of the Special Representative for Afghanistan and Pakistan in January 2010. (Reid 2010)

If the gains that Afghan women have made in the way of access to basic human rights become undone, it is very possible that Afghanistan's stability gains will unravel as well. Providing governance and essential services is an important part of any COIN operation (Sediqi 2009). The ability to administer resources efficiently, design and implement reasonable policies, and establish law and order are the core elements of governance, all of which remain largely absent from the Afghan communities (Sediqi 2009). Failed leadership, weak administration, poor payment to the government officials, and lack of control over rural areas created a gap and serious resentment between the rural population and the Afghan government because most of the social services have been particularly focused on the small portion of the urban elite (Sediqi 2009). The Afghan government has been unable to deliver basic services that people depend upon, especially to those living in the rural areas of the country (Sediqi 2009). This is problematic because, while insurgents only have to convince the populace to sympathize with them enough not to take action, the government must get the active support of the people. So, it has to provide essential services, outlets for political participation, social reform, and economic opportunity, all of which the insurgent seeks to disrupt (Hand 2007). Women in particular suffer disproportionately from absence of basic governance and essential services (Standal 2008). Addressing many of the governance-related problems affecting women in Afghanistan are critical to and re-establish the legitimacy of the Afghan government throughout the country.

Task 3--Ensure Access to Education for Girls and Women as well as Men and Boys (Development Line of Effort)

The perilous status of girls' education belies one of the greatest hopes raised when the Taliban was toppled by U.S.-led forces in 2001: the liberation of Afghanistan's women.

> More than six years since the fall of the Taliban, fewer than 30% of eligible girls are enrolled in schools, and the infrastructure is so poor that only a tiny fraction are likely to get the education they need to enjoy the fruits of emancipation. While struggling to build the new infrastructure, educators must also contend with Afghanistan's old demons: the Taliban is making a comeback in

33

several provinces and reimposing its rules. In little over a year, 130 schools have been burned, 105 students and teachers killed and 307 schools closed down because of security concerns. Many of those schools were for girls, and most of them were in the southern provinces, where a Taliban-driven insurgency has made it nearly impossible to secure the schools. For girls in much of the country, education remains a dream no more attainable now than it was under the Taliban. In the past six years, 3,500 new schools have been built across the country, but fewer than half of them have buildings. Most are in tents, in the shade of trees or wherever open space can be made available. This has a direct bearing on the number of girls enrolled: most Afghan families will not allow their daughters to be where they may be seen by men. "Girls in this society have certain needs," says Education Minister Hanif Atmar. "They cannot be in a tented school or in an open space with no sanitation facilities, so they simply do not go. (Stockman– Boston Globe)

Furthermore,

Statistics reveal that 85.1 percent of Afghani women have no formal education and, of those that attend school, an estimated 74 percent of girls drop out by the fifth grade. Nearly 79 percent of women are illiterate and only 1 percent of girls in rural communities attend school. While attendance at school for girls is currently safer than has been in the women's advocates in Afghanistan highlight that protections for women remain mostly theoretical in much of the country, particularly in rural areas, where tradition runs deepest and women have limited access to advocacy services and courts past, it is still not completely without risk of violence including death. (Women for Women International 2010)

The stakes for Afghan society are high. Every social and economic index shows

that countries with a higher percentage of women with a high school education also have

better overall health, a more functional democracy and increased economic performance.

The other payoff that is especially important to Afghanistan: educated women are a

strong bulwark against the extremism that still plagues Afghanistan. Says Ghulam Hazrat

Tanha, Herat's director of education, "Education is the factory that turns animals into

human beings. If women are educated, that means their children will be too. If the people

of the world want to solve the hard problems in Afghanistan--kidnapping, beheadings,

crime and even al-Qaeda--they should invest in [our] education" (Baker).

Furthermore, local education is critical in keeping young men under the control of their families and out of Taliban clutches. Young men generally seek permission from their mothers prior to going on Jihad, educated women tend not to give that blessing, "The persistent attacks on girls' schools indicate the threat of women's education to the Taliban strategy (Kolenda 2010).

Moreover, access to education for women and girls is important to obtain substantial empowerment that will pass the test of time, in particular obtaining knowledge, skills and information to provide human resources enhancing economic prospects (Standal 2008). An enormous constraint on the economic and political participation of Afghan women is lack of access to education and training. A huge proportion of Afghan women are simply not equipped with the skills to participate more fully in their communities (International Crisis Group 2003).

The women of Afghanistan urgently need access to economic opportunity. Already restricted from joining the formal work sector due to long-standing cultural constraints (United Nations Assistance Mission in Afghanistan 2009), their need has only become more acute through years of conflict because the loss of men and boys from households and communities due to war has increased the burden on women and girls to provide for family well being (International Crisis Group 2003). Economic growth is vital to establishing social stability, which is the ultimate objective of the Afghanistan COIN campaign (Schramm 2010). The areas of the globe that perpetuate terrorism have had low or negative growth rates over the last thirty years (Schramm 2010).

When it comes to economic investment, women are excellent candidates because not only are they more likely to be poor than men, but also because women tend to use any marginal increases in their incomes to invest in the health, nutrition, and education of their families (Coleman 2010). In fact, the investment firm Goldman Sachs created a $100 million initiative to train women from emerging economies because the company's own research demonstrated that directing resources towards women leads to greater labor-force participation, higher productivity, and higher returns in investment (Coleman 2010).

A successful Equal Opportunity COIN strategy should integrate a specific, women-centric focus into Operation Enduring Freedom's lines of operation by prioritizing some carefully thought-out stability tasks, as noted above.

CHAPTER 5

RECOMMENDATIONS FOR AN EQUAL OPPORTUNITY COUNTERINSURGENCY STRATEGY IN AFGHANISTAN

Doctrine

The U.S. Tactics in COIN manual contains a remarkable paragraph that recommends using female military and interagency actors to engage local women as a means to undermine insurgents. It summarizes the connection between women, social networks, and support for insurgents, and highlights the linkages between influencing women, children, families, and communities. (U.S. Army 2009). This paragraph is a doctrinal gem that is unfortunately buried in the annex to the manual, where it seems to have been forgotten. Doctrine-writers and COIN practitioners should make sure that this valuable doctrinal principle is highlighted and taught as part of mainstream COIN education.

Provincial Reconstruction Teams

PRTs should dedicate capacity to outreach and engagement with Afghan women's shura councils, in order to ensure that data and information gathered from the male tribal elders corresponds to the needs of women in Afghan provinces, villages, and towns. In addition, PRTs should work with the ANP and Afghan National Army to ensure that there is adequate security for women to enjoy the fruits of PRT projects.

Female Engagement Teams

The U.S. military is on-track with the new interest in FETs. The FETSs should continue to be supported at the highest levels of the military, and they should be adequately staffed and resourced. FETs should not be limited to searching women or comforting them during a clearing operation. Instead of using them exclusively in the "clearing" phase of COIN operations, they should be used more in the "holding" phase (Matt Pottinger 2010). In other words, FETs should be authorized to make recurring visits to households to create meaningful relationships and deliver lasting benefits, going beyond simply identifying women's grievances by actually helping to address them in partnership with local leaders, NGO, and Afghan police (Matt Pottinger 2010). The goodwill achieved is at risk of being lost if the FET withdraws abruptly, never to see the women again (Matt Pottinger 2010).

A common problem with FETs is that they are new, and often ad hoc in nature (Pottinger). Until recent months, virtually all FET members usually have full-time jobs in addition to their FET duties (Matt Pottinger 2010). This limits their time for training and rehearsals and thus hampers both their effectiveness and safety (Matt Pottinger 2010). The teams should be comprised of full-time members and given the intensive training and resources they need (Matt Pottinger 2010). Poorly trained FET teams can alienate communities, and a poorly trained FETs is probably worse than having no FET at all (Matt Pottinger 2010). In addition, FET team missions are dangerous. Failure to properly train, equip, and resource FET team members puts their lives at risk (Matt Pottinger 2010).

There is little literature, and no quantitative research, about the positive effects of engaging women as a COIN tactic. The new FETs should establish and maintain benchmarks to ensure that the effects of their work are quantifiable. Measureable successes will help to ensure that such programs are integrated into COIN tactics.

Security

Security remains a constant issue for the women of Afghanistan. The ANP and Afghan National Army do not represent meaningful security for Afghan women because they are often comprised of corrupt and violent personnel who continue to proliferate extremist ideology when it comes to the treatment of women. The U.S. military and Department of State should ensure that training for these forces includes modules that educate the Afghan National Army and ANP on the appropriate treatment of women and teach law enforcement principles that emphasize the International Declaration of Human Rights, the Convention on the Elimination of all forms of Discrimination Against Women, other relevant international standards, as well as Afghanistan's own constitution. In addition, the U.S. ANP police training program has not ensured there are enough women on the force (Novak 2010). Even taking into account the cultural mores that make training female police officers difficult in a male-dominated career field and country, efforts to train women have fallen woefully short (Novak 2010). While more than 172,000 Afghans completed basic and advanced training courses, only 131 are women (Novak 2010). As the Department of Defense takes on the task of training the ANP, it should address these concerns. In addition, expanding the number of Family Response Units in local police districts will enable more culturally sensitive and responsive engagement with women (Afghan Women's Network 2010).

39

Governance

Afghan activist Mariam Rawi notes that warlords holding power in the provinces were hardly advocates of the rights of women in the past, and now they are buttressed by Western support. She writes, "The war on terrorism has toppled the Taliban regime, but it has not removed religious fundamentalism, which is the main cause of misery for Afghan women. In fact, by bringing the warlords back to power, the U.S. government has replaced one misogynist fundamentalist regime with another" (Rawi 2004).

President Barack Obama's December 2009 Afghanistan and Pakistan strategy review, in which he outlined his decision to send 30,000 more troops to Afghanistan, did not reference the impact a failed U.S. effort would have on Afghan women and girls (Juul 2009). In contrast, President Obama's strategy review in March of 2009 noted, "the denial of basic human rights to the Afghan people--especially women and girls" as one of the terrible consequences of international withdrawal from Afghanistan (Juul 2009).

The U.S. military should work closely with its civilian counterparts to ensure that Afghan women are not ignored as the U.S. implements its new Afghanistan strategy. As the U.S. and the Karzai administration contemplate talks with the Taliban, the U.S. should not sacrifice the human rights and fundamental freedoms of Afghan women in order to bring the Taliban to the table. Public statements from the U.S. diplomatic and military fronts should emphasize that the U.S. will not be a part of reconciliation deals at the expense of Afghan women.

Access to Education

The education of Afghan women is a critical lynchpin in fighting insurgency. Given the early age of marriage and childbirth for Afghan women, the dividends of investing in education for Afghan girls pay out relatively quickly. In a matter of a few years, education can yield benefits that can change an entire generation's worth of perspectives. However, educating girls is not simply a matter of building schools. Infrastructure projects require local, national, and international partnerships that ensure that there are teachers, textbooks, and a curriculum to be taught. The U.S. military should partner more closely with NGO, local, and interagency partners to ensure that schools have the teachers and resources to make the project worthwhile. Further, because of the controversial nature of girls education in much of Afghanistan and the challenges associated with girls in public places, girls school infrastructure projects need to be undertaken in close consultation with both men and women in the local community so that the buildings provide adequate safety, sanitation, and privacy to make the spaces useable for females. Finally, security remains a primary constraint for girls who desire to attend school. The U.S. military should work in close coordination with the ANP to ensure a permissive security environment for girls, as well as teachers.

CHAPTER 6

CONCLUSION

<u>Equal Opportunity Counterinsurgency</u>

The Taliban and associated insurgent factions rely on the Afghan people to provide their food, money, weapons, training, shelter, and recruits. They can win this support through terror or loyalty. Either way, they depend upon the complicity of the Afghan people, who they live among as they plan their attacks against U.S. forces. This is why the U.S. strategy in Afghanistan centers on winning the loyalty of the Afghan people--convince the people to stop supporting the Taliban, and the Taliban's entire logistics base dries up. Winning this support is hard enough when the U.S. military is already perceived as a hostile foreign force. It is even harder when the U.S. military has not engaged half the population.

Though changing, the prevalent perception within the U.S. military is that Afghan women are powerless in Afghan society and therefore unimportant to the counterinsurgency campaign. The military's Female Engagement Teams that have deployed with the express purpose of building trust with Afghan women are a promising indicator of a shift in the military's thinking, but they constitute such a small fraction U.S. troops in Afghanistan that they are statistically almost irrelevant.

While many Afghan women endure severe restrictions on their movement and freedoms, they actually play a central role in village life because they bear the burden of essential tasks, like raising children, cooking, fetching water, and taking care of livestock. Experts at creating news networks that fall beneath the radars of men, Afghan women know all of the goings-on of their villages, including the presence of insurgents. Charged with the upbringing of their children, Afghan women often wield significant influence within the family, including their adolescent male sons who make up the recruiting pool of the insurgents. The Army's own counterinsurgency doctrine advises, "Win the women, and you own the family unit. Own the family, and you take a big step forward in mobilizing the population."

It stands to reason that a counterinsurgency strategy that relies on winning over the people is not going to be particularly successful if half the population never gets to interact with the counterinsurgents in the first place. This is why the U.S. military needs to ensure that its troops are "Equal Opportunity" counterinsurgents, who work to engage women as well as men.

Equal Opportunity counterinsurgents know that ignoring half the population means missing significant opportunities to gain intelligence and build trust within Afghan communities. They understand that while Afghan village elders may purport to speak for the village, these same elders come under pressure from insurgents to restrict women's freedom of movement and access to education and employment.

Equal Opportunity counterinsurgents also know that Afghan women are not tragic figures in blue burqas, but individuals with unique talents and contributions to make to their country. They understand that Afghan history proudly features women as teachers, doctors, and scientists, and that the severe limitations placed on the human rights and fundamental freedoms of women are less a characteristic of Afghan "culture" and more a consequence of thirty years of war, power politics, and targeted and violent oppression.

Equal Opportunity counterinsurgents know that if Afghan women cannot trust the Afghan National Police to protect them from rape, forced marriage, and domestic violence, they will continue to tolerate alternative guarantees from the Taliban as a better hedge for the safety and security of themselves and their children. They understand that as long as women lack access to education and economic opportunity, they will be forced into illicit industries like poppy production and prostitution, which directly fund insurgent coffers.

Finally, Equal Opportunity counterinsurgents understand the link between the security of women and the security of nations. As the security environment continues to erode for Afghan women, so too erodes the credibility of Afghanistan's central government, whose legitimacy rests on its ability to provide governance, rule of law and security for all Afghans. Equal Opportunity counterinsurgents understand that, as long as violence and insecurity rule the lives of Afghan women, violence and insecurity will rule in Afghanistan. The resulting instability creates space for insurgents and their terrorist allies to thrive, which has national security consequences for the United States.

REFERENCE LIST

Afghan Women's Network. 2007. *Operationalizing gender in provincial reconstruction teams in Afghanistan.* 1 August. http://www.afghanwomensnetwork.org/advocacyDetail.php?resId=45 (accessed 20 May 2010).

———. 2010. *UNIFEM.* 27 January. http://www.unifem.org/news_events/story_detail.php?StoryID=1020 (accessed 21 May 2010).

Bernard, Cheryl. 2002. *Veiled courage: Inside the Afghan women's resistence.* New York: Broadway Books.

Bumiller, Elisabeth. 2010. *The New York Times Online.* 6 March. http://www.nytimes.com/2010/03/07/world/asia/07women.html (accessed 21 May 2010).

Chiarelli, Peter W. 2005. Winning the peace: The Requirement For Full Spectrum Operations. *Military Review* (July/August).

Clark, Kate. 2006. *New statesman.* 27 November. http://www.newstatesman.com/200611270015 (accessed 21 May 2010).

Clinton, Hillary. 2009. *Opening remarks before the House Foreign Affairs Committee.* Washington, DC: House Foreign Affairs Committee, 2 December.

Coleman, Isabel. 2010. The better half: Helping women help the world. *Foreign Affairs* (January/February): 126-130.

Crews, Robert D. 2008. *The Taliban and the crisis of Afghanistan.* Cambridge: Harvard University Press.

Darius, 2nd Lt. Christine. 2010. Governor, ISAF develop priorities for Afghan women in Farah. *www.isaf.nato.int.* 30 May. http://www.isaf.nato.int/article/isaf-releases/efforts-to-empower-afghan-women-in-farah.html (accessed 31 May 2010).

Davidson, Janine. 2007. Al Qaeda as intervenor or insurgent. In *Countering Insurgency and Promoting Democracy,* by Manolis Priniotakis, 157. New York: Council for Emerging National Security Affairs.

Grau, Lester W. 2010. Interview by author, Ft Leavenworth, KS. 14 May.

Hand, Bailey. 2007. Core components of insurgency and counterinsurgency theory. In *Countering Insurgency and Promoting Democracy,* by Manolis Priniotakis, 20. New York: Council for Emerging National Security Affairs.

45

Hudson, Valerie M., and Patricial Leidl. 2010. *Foreign Policy.* 10 May. http://www.foreignpolicy.com/articles/2010/05/07/the_us_is_abandoning_afghanistan_s_women (accessed 21 May 2010).

International Crisis Group. 2003. http://www.crisisgroup.org/en/ regions/asia/south-asia/afghanistan/048-afghanistan-women-and-reconstruction.aspx (accessed 21 May 2010).

International Security Forces Afghanistan. 2010. http://www.isaf.nato.int/en/ article/isaf-releases/frontline-females-unlocking-the-world-of-afghan-women.html (accessed 21 May 2010).

Jibril, MAJ Mona. 2006. Director of the Non-Governmental Assistance Center, Iraq. Interview by Dr. Neil Rogers. 20 December.

Jones, Ann. 2009. Remember the women? *The Nation* (9 November): 22-26.

Juul, Peter. 2009. Afghan Women still need U.S. support. *Center for American Progress.* 14 December. http://webcache.googleusercontent.com/ search?q=cache:J-7IzjGz0rcJ:www.americanprogress.org/issues/2009/12/ afghan_womens_rights.html+women+forced+to+support+taliban+for+security&cd=10&hl=en&ct=clnk&gl=us&client=safari (accessed 25 May 2010).

Krawchuk, Fred. 2007. The integral role of strategic communication n counterinsurgency operations. In *Countering Insurgency and Promoting Democracy*, by Manolis Priniotakis, 263. New York: Council for Emerging National Security Affairs.

Lawrence, Chris. 2010. Going where male marines can't. *cnn.com.* 1 April. http://afghanistan.blogs.cnn.com/2010/04/01/going-where-male-marines-cant/ (accessed 29 May 2010).

Latty, Melissa A. 2009. *Marines.mil.* 12 June. http://www.marines.mil/unit/2ndmlg/ hq/Pages/LionessesworktoimprovecommunityinlocalIraqcity.aspx (accessed 21 May 2010).

Mao Tse-Tung, Samuel B Griffith. *Mao Tse-Tung on guerrilla warfare.* Chicago: University of Illinois Press.

Malevich, JJ. 2009. *USA and USMC counterinsurgency center blog.* 4 December. http://usacac.leavenworth.army.mil/blog/blogs/coin/default.aspx (accessed 21 May 2010).

Matt Pottinger, Hali Jilani, and Claire Russo. 2010. Half-hearted: trying to win Afghanistan without Afghan Women. *Small Wars Journal*: 1-10.

Novak, Lisa M. 2010. *Stars and Stripes.* 25 February. http://www.stripes.com/ article.asp?section=104&article=68304 (accessed 21 May 2010).

Perito, Robert M. 2005. *The U.S. experience with provincial reconstruction teams in Afghanistan: Lessons identified.* Special Report. Washington, DC: United States Institute for Peace.

Pilch, Francis. 2006. The potential role of women in contributing to countering ideological support for terrorism: The cases of Bosnia and Afghanistan. *Connections, the Quarterly Journal* (September): 107.

Pottinger, Mark. 2009. *Female engagement team after action review and way forward.* AAR, United States Marine Corps.

Qayoumi, Mohammad. 2010. Once upon a time in Afghanistan. *Foreign Policy.* 27 May. http://www.foreignpolicy.com/articles/2010/05/27/once_upon_a_time_in_ afghanistan (accessed 31 May 2010).

Rawi, Miriam. 2004. Betrayal. *Reproductive Health Matters* (January): 116-125.

Ree, Foon. 2009. *Boston globe.* 23 April. http://www.boston.com/news/nation/articles/ 2009/04/24/afghan_veterans_offer_stories_from_7_year_us_involvement/ (accessed 21 May 2010).

Reid, Rachel. 2010. *Human rights watch.* 24 February. http://www.hrw.org/en/news/ 2010/02/24/testimony-rachel-reid-senate-foreign-relations-committee (accessed 21 May 2010).

Revolutionary Association of the Women of Afghanistan. January 1997. http://www.rawa.org/index.php (accessed 21 May 2010).

Rice, Condoleezza. 2006. *Independent women's forum.* 14 May. http://www.iwf.org/ news/show/19071.html (accessed 21 May 2010).

Ricks, Tom. 2009. *Foreign policy.* 9 October. http://ricks.foreignpolicy.com/posts/ 2009/10/09/women_in_coin_ii_how_to_do_it_right (accessed 21 May 2010).

Roberts, M. E. 2005. *Villages of the moon: Psychological operations in Southern Afghanistan.* Baltimore: Publish America.

Schramm, Carl J. 2010. Expeditionary economics: Spurring growth after conflicts and disasters. *Foreign Affairs* (May/June): 89-99.

Sediqi, Fawad. 2009. Why are the Taliban still a challenge for the Afghan government and the international community after their removal from power? Masters Thesis, Canterbury: University of Kent.

Sennott, C.M. 2009. Life, death, and the Taliban. *Global Post*, 30 July. http://www.globalpost.com/taliban/coin (accessed 21 May 2010).

Skaine, Rosemarie. 2002. *The women of Afghanistan under the Taliban.* Jefferson, NC: McFarland and Company.

Standal, Karina. 2008. Giving light and hope in rural Afghanistan. Master's Thesis, Oslo: University of Oslo.

Sutten, MAJ Marne L. 2009. The rising importance of women in terrorism and the need to reform counterterrorism strategy. Monograph, School of Advanced Military Studies, Ft. Leavenworth.

Tyson, Ann Scott. 2009. *Washington Post Online.* 7 May. http://www.washington post.com/wp-dyn/content/article/2009/05/07/AR2009050704239.html (accessed 21 May 2010).

United Nations Assistance Mission in Afghanistan. 2009. *Silence is violence: End the abuse of women in Afghanistan.* Assessment, United Nations Assistance Mission in Afghanistan, Geneva: Office of the United Nations High Commissioner for Human Rights.

United Nations Development Fund for Women. 2004. Afghanistan unveiled. *Public Broadcasting Service.* 17 November.. http://www.pbs.org/independentlens/ afghanistanunveiled/women.html (accessed 31 May 2010).

United States Marine Corps Center for Lessons Learned. 2009. *Operations in Afghanistan: Lessons from 2007-2009.* Ft. Belvoir: United States Marine Corps Center for Lessons Learned.

U.S. Army. 2006. Field Manual (FM) 3-24, *Counterinsurgency.* Ft. Leavenworth: Government Printing Office.

U.S. Army. 2009. Field Manual (FM) 3-24.2, *Tactics in counterinsurgency.* Ft. Leavenworth: Government Printing Office.

www.ingramcontent.com/pod-product-compliance
Lightning Source LLC
Chambersburg PA
CBHW080609290526
45790CB00007B/2707